50 Family Dinner Recipes

By: Kelly Johnson

Table of Contents

- Classic Meatloaf
- Chicken Alfredo Pasta
- Beef Stroganoff
- Baked Ziti
- Slow Cooker Pot Roast
- Chicken Parmesan
- Homemade Sloppy Joes
- Shepherd's Pie
- BBQ Pulled Pork Sandwiches
- Stuffed Bell Peppers
- Chicken and Rice Casserole
- Spaghetti and Meatballs
- Honey Garlic Salmon
- Vegetarian Chili
- Chicken Fajitas
- Beef and Broccoli Stir-Fry
- Turkey and Spinach Lasagna
- Creamy Tuscan Chicken
- Cajun Shrimp and Grits
- One-Pan Lemon Garlic Chicken
- Homemade Mac and Cheese
- Teriyaki Chicken with Rice
- Loaded Baked Potatoes
- Chicken Pot Pie
- Swedish Meatballs
- Balsamic Glazed Pork Chops
- Vegetable Stir-Fry with Tofu
- Cheeseburger Sliders
- Chicken Enchiladas
- Greek Chicken Gyros
- Classic Beef Tacos
- Shrimp Scampi
- Mushroom Risotto
- BBQ Chicken Pizza
- Baked Lemon Herb Cod

- Meatball Subs
- Chicken Marsala
- Sausage and Peppers
- Garlic Butter Steak Bites
- Gnocchi with Pesto Sauce
- Chicken and Dumplings
- Grilled Teriyaki Pork Chops
- Beef Burrito Bowls
- Chicken and Broccoli Casserole
- Sweet and Sour Chicken
- Hawaiian BBQ Chicken
- Tuna Casserole
- Spinach and Ricotta Stuffed Shells
- Classic Jambalaya
- Pesto Pasta with Grilled Chicken

Classic Meatloaf

Ingredients:

- 1 ½ lbs ground beef (80/20 mix)
- ¾ cup breadcrumbs (plain or seasoned)
- ½ cup milk
- 1 small onion, finely chopped
- 2 cloves garlic, minced
- 1 egg
- 2 tbsp ketchup
- 1 tbsp Worcestershire sauce
- 1 tsp salt
- ½ tsp black pepper
- ½ tsp dried oregano
- ½ tsp paprika

For the Glaze:

- ¼ cup ketchup
- 1 tbsp brown sugar
- 1 tsp Worcestershire sauce

Instructions:

1. **Preheat Oven:** Set to **375°F (190°C)** and grease a loaf pan or line with parchment paper.
2. **Mix Ingredients:** In a large bowl, combine **ground beef, breadcrumbs, milk, onion, garlic, egg, ketchup, Worcestershire sauce, salt, pepper, oregano, and paprika**. Mix until just combined—avoid overmixing.
3. **Shape the Loaf:** Transfer the mixture to the loaf pan, shaping it evenly.
4. **Prepare the Glaze:** In a small bowl, mix **ketchup, brown sugar, and Worcestershire sauce**. Spread half of the glaze over the top of the meatloaf.
5. **Bake:** Place in the oven and bake for **45 minutes**. Remove, spread the remaining glaze, and bake for another **15 minutes**, or until the internal temperature reaches **160°F (71°C)**.
6. **Rest & Serve:** Let it rest for **10 minutes** before slicing. Serve warm with mashed potatoes and vegetables.

Chicken Alfredo Pasta

Ingredients:

- 12 oz fettuccine pasta
- 2 tbsp butter
- 2 cloves garlic, minced
- 2 boneless, skinless chicken breasts, sliced
- 1 cup heavy cream
- 1 cup grated Parmesan cheese
- ½ cup whole milk
- Salt & pepper to taste
- ¼ tsp nutmeg (optional)
- Fresh parsley for garnish

Instructions:

1. Cook fettuccine pasta according to package instructions; drain and set aside.
2. In a skillet, melt butter over medium heat. Add garlic and sauté for 30 seconds.
3. Add chicken slices, season with salt and pepper, and cook until golden and fully cooked.
4. Reduce heat to low and pour in heavy cream and milk. Stir in Parmesan cheese until smooth.
5. Add cooked pasta to the sauce, toss to coat, and let it simmer for 2 minutes.
6. Garnish with fresh parsley and serve warm.

Beef Stroganoff

Ingredients:

- 1 lb beef sirloin or tenderloin, sliced into thin strips
- 2 tbsp butter
- 1 small onion, chopped
- 2 cloves garlic, minced
- 8 oz mushrooms, sliced
- 1 cup beef broth
- 1 tbsp Worcestershire sauce
- 1 cup sour cream
- 1 tbsp Dijon mustard
- Salt & pepper to taste
- 8 oz egg noodles, cooked
- Fresh parsley for garnish

Instructions:

1. Heat butter in a large skillet over medium heat. Add onions and garlic, sauté until soft.
2. Add beef strips, season with salt and pepper, and cook until browned. Remove and set aside.
3. In the same skillet, add mushrooms and cook until tender.
4. Pour in beef broth and Worcestershire sauce. Let it simmer for 5 minutes.
5. Stir in sour cream and Dijon mustard, then return the beef to the skillet. Simmer for 5 minutes.
6. Serve over egg noodles and garnish with parsley.

Baked Ziti

Ingredients:

- 12 oz ziti pasta
- 1 lb ground beef or Italian sausage
- 1 small onion, chopped
- 2 cloves garlic, minced
- 24 oz marinara sauce
- 1 tsp Italian seasoning
- 1 cup ricotta cheese
- 1 cup shredded mozzarella cheese
- ½ cup grated Parmesan cheese
- Salt & pepper to taste

Instructions:

1. Preheat oven to 375°F (190°C).
2. Cook ziti pasta according to package instructions; drain and set aside.
3. In a skillet, cook ground beef with onions and garlic until browned. Drain excess fat.
4. Add marinara sauce and Italian seasoning, simmer for 5 minutes.
5. In a baking dish, layer half of the cooked pasta, half of the meat sauce, and dollops of ricotta cheese. Repeat layers.
6. Top with mozzarella and Parmesan cheese.
7. Bake uncovered for 25 minutes until cheese is melted and bubbly.
8. Let it cool slightly before serving.

Slow Cooker Pot Roast

Ingredients:

- 3 lb beef chuck roast
- 1 tbsp olive oil
- 1 tsp salt
- ½ tsp black pepper
- 1 tsp garlic powder
- 1 onion, sliced
- 3 carrots, chopped
- 3 potatoes, cubed
- 2 cups beef broth
- 1 tbsp Worcestershire sauce
- 1 tsp dried thyme
- 1 tsp dried rosemary

Instructions:

1. Heat olive oil in a skillet over medium-high heat. Season roast with salt, pepper, and garlic powder. Sear on all sides until browned.
2. Place onions, carrots, and potatoes in the bottom of the slow cooker.
3. Place the seared roast on top and pour in beef broth and Worcestershire sauce. Sprinkle with thyme and rosemary.
4. Cover and cook on **low for 8 hours** or **high for 4-5 hours** until the meat is tender.
5. Remove roast, shred or slice, and serve with vegetables and broth.

Chicken Parmesan

Ingredients:

- 2 boneless, skinless chicken breasts
- ½ cup flour
- 2 eggs, beaten
- 1 cup breadcrumbs
- ½ cup grated Parmesan cheese
- 1 tsp Italian seasoning
- 1 cup marinara sauce
- 1 cup shredded mozzarella cheese
- 2 tbsp olive oil
- Salt & pepper to taste

Instructions:

1. Preheat oven to **375°F (190°C)**.
2. Pound chicken breasts to even thickness, season with salt and pepper.
3. Dredge in flour, dip in beaten eggs, then coat with breadcrumbs mixed with Parmesan and Italian seasoning.
4. Heat olive oil in a skillet over medium heat and cook chicken until golden brown on both sides.
5. Transfer to a baking dish, top with marinara sauce and mozzarella cheese.
6. Bake for **20 minutes** until cheese is melted. Serve with pasta or salad.

Homemade Sloppy Joes

Ingredients:

- 1 lb ground beef
- ½ cup chopped onion
- ½ cup chopped green bell pepper
- 2 cloves garlic, minced
- 1 cup tomato sauce
- ¼ cup ketchup
- 1 tbsp Worcestershire sauce
- 1 tbsp brown sugar
- ½ tsp salt
- ½ tsp black pepper
- 4 hamburger buns

Instructions:

1. In a skillet, cook ground beef over medium heat until browned. Drain excess fat.
2. Add onion, bell pepper, and garlic, cook until softened.
3. Stir in tomato sauce, ketchup, Worcestershire sauce, brown sugar, salt, and pepper. Simmer for **10 minutes**.
4. Serve on toasted hamburger buns.

Shepherd's Pie

Ingredients:

- 1 lb ground lamb (or beef)
- 1 small onion, chopped
- 2 cloves garlic, minced
- 1 cup frozen mixed vegetables
- 1 tbsp tomato paste
- 1 cup beef broth
- 1 tsp Worcestershire sauce
- 4 cups mashed potatoes
- ½ cup shredded cheddar cheese
- Salt & pepper to taste

Instructions:

1. Preheat oven to **375°F (190°C)**.
2. In a skillet, cook ground meat, onion, and garlic until browned. Drain excess fat.
3. Stir in tomato paste, beef broth, Worcestershire sauce, and vegetables. Simmer for **5 minutes**.
4. Transfer to a baking dish, top with mashed potatoes and sprinkle with cheese.
5. Bake for **20 minutes** until golden.

BBQ Pulled Pork Sandwiches

Ingredients:

- 3 lb pork shoulder
- 1 cup BBQ sauce
- 1 onion, sliced
- 1 cup chicken broth
- 1 tsp garlic powder
- 1 tsp smoked paprika
- Salt & pepper to taste
- 4 sandwich buns

Instructions:

1. Place pork, onion, chicken broth, and seasonings in a **slow cooker**. Cook on **low for 8 hours**.
2. Shred pork with two forks, mix with BBQ sauce.
3. Serve on sandwich buns with coleslaw.

Stuffed Bell Peppers

Ingredients:

- 4 large bell peppers
- 1 lb ground beef (or turkey)
- 1 small onion, chopped
- 1 cup cooked rice
- 1 cup marinara sauce
- ½ cup shredded cheese
- 1 tsp Italian seasoning
- Salt & pepper to taste

Instructions:

1. Preheat oven to **375°F (190°C)**.
2. Cut tops off peppers, remove seeds.
3. In a skillet, cook ground beef and onion until browned. Stir in rice, marinara sauce, and seasoning.
4. Stuff peppers with mixture, place in a baking dish.
5. Cover with foil and bake for **30 minutes**. Remove foil, top with cheese, and bake for **10 more minutes**.

Chicken and Rice Casserole

Ingredients:

- 2 boneless, skinless chicken breasts
- 1 cup rice
- 1 ½ cups chicken broth
- 1 cup cream of mushroom (or cream of chicken) soup
- 1 cup shredded cheddar cheese
- ½ tsp garlic powder
- Salt & pepper to taste

Instructions:

1. Preheat oven to **375°F (190°C)**.
2. Mix rice, chicken broth, soup, and seasonings in a baking dish.
3. Place chicken breasts on top, cover with foil.
4. Bake for **40 minutes**, remove foil, top with cheese, and bake for **10 more minutes**.

Spaghetti and Meatballs

Ingredients:

- 12 oz spaghetti
- 1 lb ground beef
- ½ cup breadcrumbs
- 1 egg
- ½ tsp garlic powder
- ½ tsp salt
- 1 jar marinara sauce
- 2 tbsp olive oil

Instructions:

1. Cook spaghetti according to package directions.
2. Mix ground beef, breadcrumbs, egg, garlic powder, and salt. Shape into meatballs.
3. Heat olive oil in a pan, cook meatballs until browned.
4. Add marinara sauce, simmer for **15 minutes**. Serve over spaghetti.

Honey Garlic Salmon

Ingredients:

- 2 salmon fillets
- 2 tbsp honey
- 2 tbsp soy sauce
- 1 tsp minced garlic
- 1 tsp lemon juice

Instructions:

1. Mix honey, soy sauce, garlic, and lemon juice.
2. Marinate salmon for **15 minutes**.
3. Cook in a skillet over medium heat for **3-4 minutes per side**.

Vegetarian Chili

Ingredients:

- 1 can black beans, drained
- 1 can kidney beans, drained
- 1 can diced tomatoes
- 1 cup corn
- 1 small onion, chopped
- 2 cloves garlic, minced
- 1 tsp cumin
- 1 tsp chili powder

Instructions:

1. In a pot, sauté onion and garlic until soft.
2. Add beans, tomatoes, corn, and seasonings. Simmer for **20 minutes**.

Chicken Fajitas

Ingredients:

- 2 boneless, skinless chicken breasts, sliced
- 1 red bell pepper, sliced
- 1 green bell pepper, sliced
- 1 onion, sliced
- 1 tbsp olive oil
- 1 tsp cumin
- 1 tsp chili powder
- 4 flour tortillas

Instructions:

1. Heat oil in a skillet, cook chicken until golden.
2. Add peppers, onion, and seasonings. Cook for **5 minutes**.
3. Serve in tortillas with toppings of choice.

Beef and Broccoli Stir-Fry

Ingredients:

- 1 lb flank steak, sliced thin
- 2 cups broccoli florets
- 2 tbsp soy sauce
- 1 tbsp oyster sauce
- 1 tsp garlic, minced
- 1 tsp ginger, minced
- 1 tbsp cornstarch
- 1 tbsp sesame oil

Instructions:

1. Toss beef with soy sauce and cornstarch.
2. Heat sesame oil in a pan, cook beef until browned. Remove.
3. Add garlic, ginger, and broccoli. Stir-fry for **3 minutes**.
4. Return beef, add oyster sauce, cook for **2 more minutes**. Serve over rice.

Turkey and Spinach Lasagna

Ingredients:

- 9 lasagna noodles, cooked
- 1 lb ground turkey
- 1 small onion, chopped
- 2 cloves garlic, minced
- 1 (24 oz) jar marinara sauce
- 2 cups fresh spinach, chopped
- 1 (15 oz) container ricotta cheese
- 1 egg
- 1 tsp Italian seasoning
- 2 cups shredded mozzarella cheese
- ½ cup grated Parmesan cheese

Instructions:

1. Preheat oven to **375°F (190°C)**.
2. In a skillet, cook turkey, onion, and garlic until browned. Stir in marinara sauce and spinach.
3. In a bowl, mix ricotta, egg, and Italian seasoning.
4. Layer a baking dish with sauce, noodles, and ricotta mixture. Repeat layers, ending with sauce and mozzarella cheese.
5. Sprinkle Parmesan on top and bake for **40 minutes** until bubbly.

Creamy Tuscan Chicken

Ingredients:

- 2 boneless, skinless chicken breasts
- 2 tbsp olive oil
- 2 cloves garlic, minced
- 1 cup heavy cream
- ½ cup chicken broth
- ½ cup sun-dried tomatoes, chopped
- 1 cup spinach
- ½ cup grated Parmesan cheese
- Salt & pepper to taste

Instructions:

1. Heat olive oil in a skillet over medium heat. Season chicken with salt & pepper, cook until golden. Remove and set aside.
2. Sauté garlic, then add heavy cream, broth, sun-dried tomatoes, and Parmesan. Simmer for **5 minutes**.
3. Stir in spinach and return chicken to the skillet. Cook for **5 more minutes**.

Cajun Shrimp and Grits

Ingredients:

- 1 lb shrimp, peeled & deveined
- 1 tsp Cajun seasoning
- 1 tbsp butter
- 1 cup grits
- 3 cups water
- ½ cup shredded cheddar cheese
- ½ cup heavy cream
- 1 green onion, chopped

Instructions:

1. Bring water to a boil, stir in grits, and cook until thick. Add cheese and heavy cream.
2. Season shrimp with Cajun seasoning and sauté in butter for **3 minutes** per side.
3. Serve shrimp over grits, garnished with green onions.

One-Pan Lemon Garlic Chicken

Ingredients:

- 2 boneless, skinless chicken breasts
- 1 tbsp olive oil
- 2 cloves garlic, minced
- 1 tsp lemon zest
- 1 tbsp lemon juice
- ½ tsp dried oregano
- Salt & pepper to taste
- 1 cup broccoli florets

Instructions:

1. Heat oil in a skillet, cook chicken until golden.
2. Add garlic, lemon juice, zest, and oregano. Sauté for **2 minutes**.
3. Add broccoli, cover, and cook for **5 more minutes**.

Homemade Mac and Cheese

Ingredients:

- 8 oz elbow macaroni
- 2 tbsp butter
- 2 tbsp flour
- 2 cups milk
- 2 cups shredded cheddar cheese
- ½ tsp mustard powder
- Salt & pepper to taste

Instructions:

1. Cook macaroni according to package instructions.
2. In a saucepan, melt butter, whisk in flour, and cook for **1 minute**.
3. Gradually add milk, whisking until thick. Stir in cheese, mustard powder, salt, and pepper.
4. Mix sauce with pasta and serve warm.

Teriyaki Chicken with Rice

Ingredients:

- 2 boneless, skinless chicken breasts
- ¼ cup soy sauce
- 2 tbsp honey
- 1 tbsp rice vinegar
- 1 tsp garlic, minced
- 1 tsp ginger, grated
- 1 cup cooked rice
- 1 tbsp sesame seeds

Instructions:

1. Mix soy sauce, honey, vinegar, garlic, and ginger.
2. Marinate chicken for **30 minutes**, then cook in a skillet until done.
3. Serve over rice, garnished with sesame seeds.

Loaded Baked Potatoes

Ingredients:

- 4 large russet potatoes
- 1 cup shredded cheddar cheese
- ½ cup sour cream
- 4 slices bacon, cooked & crumbled
- 2 green onions, chopped
- 2 tbsp butter

Instructions:

1. Preheat oven to **400°F (200°C)**. Poke potatoes with a fork and bake for **50 minutes**.
2. Slice open, fluff insides with a fork, and mix with butter.
3. Top with cheese, sour cream, bacon, and green onions.

Chicken Pot Pie

Ingredients:

- 2 boneless, skinless chicken breasts, cooked & shredded
- 1 cup mixed vegetables
- 1 cup chicken broth
- 1 cup heavy cream
- 2 tbsp flour
- 2 tbsp butter
- 1 refrigerated pie crust

Instructions:

1. Preheat oven to **375°F (190°C)**.
2. Melt butter in a pan, stir in flour, then add broth and cream. Simmer until thick.
3. Stir in chicken and vegetables. Transfer to a baking dish.
4. Cover with pie crust, cut slits, and bake for **30 minutes**.

Swedish Meatballs

Ingredients:

- 1 lb ground beef
- ½ cup breadcrumbs
- 1 egg
- ½ tsp nutmeg
- ½ tsp allspice
- 1 cup beef broth
- ½ cup heavy cream
- 1 tbsp flour
- 1 tbsp butter

Instructions:

1. Mix beef, breadcrumbs, egg, nutmeg, and allspice. Shape into meatballs.
2. Brown meatballs in a skillet, remove, and set aside.
3. In the same pan, melt butter, whisk in flour, then add broth and cream. Simmer until thick.
4. Return meatballs and cook for **5 minutes**. Serve with mashed potatoes.

Balsamic Glazed Pork Chops

Ingredients:

- 4 pork chops
- ½ cup balsamic vinegar
- 2 tbsp honey
- 1 tbsp Dijon mustard
- 2 cloves garlic, minced
- Salt & pepper to taste

Instructions:

1. Season pork chops with salt & pepper.
2. In a skillet, cook pork chops for **4 minutes per side**.
3. Mix vinegar, honey, mustard, and garlic. Pour over pork, cook for **2 minutes** until glazed.

Vegetable Stir-Fry with Tofu

Ingredients:

- 1 block firm tofu, cubed
- 2 tbsp soy sauce
- 1 tbsp sesame oil
- 1 cup broccoli florets
- 1 red bell pepper, sliced
- 1 carrot, julienned
- 1 zucchini, sliced
- 2 cloves garlic, minced
- 1 tbsp cornstarch mixed with 2 tbsp water (for thickening)
- ½ tsp ginger, grated

Instructions:

1. Heat sesame oil in a pan and cook tofu until golden brown. Remove and set aside.
2. Add garlic and ginger, then stir-fry vegetables for **5 minutes**.
3. Stir in soy sauce and cornstarch mixture. Add tofu back and cook for **2 more minutes**.

Cheeseburger Sliders

Ingredients:

- 1 lb ground beef
- ½ tsp salt & pepper
- ½ tsp garlic powder
- 6 slider buns
- 6 slices cheddar cheese
- ¼ cup diced onions
- ¼ cup pickles
- 2 tbsp ketchup

Instructions:

1. Shape beef into small patties and season with salt, pepper, and garlic powder.
2. Cook patties on a skillet for **3 minutes per side**.
3. Place cheese on patties and let melt. Assemble sliders with onions, pickles, and ketchup.

Chicken Enchiladas

Ingredients:

- 2 cups cooked, shredded chicken
- 1 cup enchilada sauce
- 1 cup shredded cheddar cheese
- ½ cup sour cream
- 6 flour tortillas
- 1 tsp cumin
- ½ tsp chili powder

Instructions:

1. Preheat oven to **375°F (190°C)**.
2. Mix chicken, ½ cup enchilada sauce, sour cream, cumin, and chili powder.
3. Fill tortillas with the mixture, roll them up, and place in a baking dish.
4. Pour remaining sauce over, sprinkle cheese, and bake for **20 minutes**.

Greek Chicken Gyros

Ingredients:

- 2 boneless chicken breasts, sliced
- 1 tbsp olive oil
- 1 tsp oregano
- ½ tsp garlic powder
- 4 pita breads
- ½ cup tzatziki sauce
- ½ cup diced tomatoes
- ½ cup sliced cucumbers
- ¼ cup red onion, sliced

Instructions:

1. Marinate chicken with olive oil, oregano, and garlic powder. Cook in a skillet for **5 minutes per side**.
2. Fill pita bread with chicken, tzatziki, tomatoes, cucumbers, and red onions.

Classic Beef Tacos

Ingredients:

- 1 lb ground beef
- 1 packet taco seasoning
- 8 small taco shells
- 1 cup shredded lettuce
- ½ cup diced tomatoes
- ½ cup shredded cheese
- ¼ cup sour cream

Instructions:

1. Cook beef in a skillet until browned. Stir in taco seasoning and **½ cup water**, simmer for **5 minutes**.
2. Fill taco shells with beef, lettuce, tomatoes, cheese, and sour cream.

Shrimp Scampi

Ingredients:

- 1 lb shrimp, peeled & deveined
- 3 tbsp butter
- 3 cloves garlic, minced
- ½ cup white wine or chicken broth
- 1 tbsp lemon juice
- 8 oz spaghetti, cooked
- ¼ tsp red pepper flakes
- ¼ cup chopped parsley

Instructions:

1. Melt butter in a skillet, add garlic, and sauté for **1 minute**.
2. Add shrimp, cook for **2 minutes per side**. Pour in wine and lemon juice, simmer for **2 minutes**.
3. Toss shrimp with pasta and top with parsley.

Mushroom Risotto

Ingredients:

- 1 cup Arborio rice
- 2 tbsp butter
- ½ onion, diced
- 2 cups mushrooms, sliced
- ½ cup white wine
- 4 cups chicken or vegetable broth
- ½ cup Parmesan cheese
- Salt & pepper to taste

Instructions:

1. Heat butter in a pot, cook onions and mushrooms until soft.
2. Add rice, stir for **1 minute**, then pour in wine and cook until absorbed.
3. Gradually add broth, stirring constantly, until rice is creamy.
4. Stir in Parmesan, season with salt & pepper.

BBQ Chicken Pizza

Ingredients:

- 1 pizza crust
- 1 cup cooked, shredded chicken
- ½ cup BBQ sauce
- 1 cup shredded mozzarella cheese
- ¼ cup red onion, sliced
- ¼ cup chopped cilantro

Instructions:

1. Preheat oven to **400°F (200°C)**.
2. Spread BBQ sauce on crust, then top with chicken, cheese, and onions.
3. Bake for **12 minutes**, then sprinkle with cilantro before serving.

Baked Lemon Herb Cod

Ingredients:

- 4 cod fillets
- 2 tbsp olive oil
- 1 tbsp lemon juice
- 1 tsp dried oregano
- ½ tsp garlic powder
- Salt & pepper to taste

Instructions:

1. Preheat oven to **375°F (190°C)**.
2. Mix olive oil, lemon juice, oregano, and garlic powder. Rub onto cod.
3. Bake for **15 minutes** until flaky.

Meatball Subs

Ingredients:

- 12 small meatballs, cooked
- 1 cup marinara sauce
- 4 hoagie rolls
- 1 cup shredded mozzarella cheese

Instructions:

1. Preheat oven to **375°F (190°C)**.
2. Heat meatballs in marinara sauce.
3. Place meatballs into hoagie rolls, top with cheese, and bake for **10 minutes**.

Chicken Marsala

Ingredients:

- 2 boneless chicken breasts
- ½ cup flour
- 1 tbsp olive oil
- 1 cup mushrooms, sliced
- ½ cup Marsala wine
- ½ cup chicken broth
- 2 tbsp butter

Instructions:

1. Dredge chicken in flour and cook in olive oil for **4 minutes per side**. Remove from pan.
2. Sauté mushrooms, then add wine and broth. Simmer for **5 minutes**.
3. Return chicken to the pan, cook for **5 more minutes**. Stir in butter before serving.

Sausage and Peppers

Ingredients:

- 1 lb Italian sausage (mild or spicy)
- 1 red bell pepper, sliced
- 1 green bell pepper, sliced
- 1 yellow onion, sliced
- 2 cloves garlic, minced
- 1 can (14.5 oz) diced tomatoes
- 1 tbsp olive oil
- 1 tsp Italian seasoning
- ½ tsp salt
- ½ tsp black pepper
- ½ tsp red pepper flakes (optional)

Instructions:

1. Heat olive oil in a large skillet over **medium heat**. Cook sausages until browned on all sides. Remove and set aside.
2. In the same skillet, sauté onions and bell peppers for **5 minutes**, until soft.
3. Add garlic, diced tomatoes, Italian seasoning, salt, black pepper, and red pepper flakes. Stir well.
4. Slice the sausages and return them to the skillet. Simmer for **10 minutes**.
5. Serve over rice, pasta, or in a hoagie roll.

Garlic Butter Steak Bites

Ingredients:

- 1 lb sirloin steak, cut into bite-sized cubes
- 3 tbsp butter
- 3 cloves garlic, minced
- 1 tbsp olive oil
- ½ tsp salt
- ½ tsp black pepper
- ½ tsp paprika
- ½ tsp red pepper flakes (optional)
- 1 tbsp chopped parsley (for garnish)

Instructions:

1. Heat olive oil in a large skillet over **medium-high heat**.
2. Season steak bites with salt, pepper, and paprika.
3. Add steak to the skillet and cook for **3-4 minutes**, stirring occasionally, until browned.
4. Reduce heat to **medium-low**, add butter and garlic, and cook for **1 more minute**.
5. Sprinkle with parsley and serve hot with mashed potatoes or steamed vegetables.

Gnocchi with Pesto Sauce

Ingredients:

- 1 lb potato gnocchi
- ½ cup basil pesto
- ¼ cup Parmesan cheese, grated
- 1 tbsp olive oil
- ½ cup cherry tomatoes, halved
- ½ cup baby spinach (optional)
- ¼ tsp salt
- ¼ tsp black pepper

Instructions:

1. Cook gnocchi according to package instructions. Drain and set aside.
2. Heat olive oil in a pan over **medium heat**. Add cherry tomatoes and spinach (if using) and cook for **2 minutes**.
3. Stir in cooked gnocchi and pesto. Toss until well coated.
4. Season with salt and black pepper. Sprinkle with Parmesan and serve warm.

Chicken and Dumplings

Ingredients:

- 1 lb boneless, skinless chicken breast, cubed
- 1 small onion, chopped
- 2 carrots, sliced
- 2 celery stalks, sliced
- 3 cloves garlic, minced
- 4 cups chicken broth
- 1 cup heavy cream
- 1 tsp thyme
- ½ tsp salt
- ½ tsp black pepper
- 1 tbsp olive oil

For the Dumplings:

- 1 cup all-purpose flour
- 2 tsp baking powder
- ½ tsp salt
- ½ cup milk
- 2 tbsp butter, melted

Instructions:

1. Heat olive oil in a pot over **medium heat**. Cook chicken until lightly browned. Remove and set aside.
2. In the same pot, sauté onion, carrots, celery, and garlic for **5 minutes**.
3. Pour in chicken broth, thyme, salt, and pepper. Bring to a boil, then reduce heat.
4. Return chicken to the pot and stir in heavy cream. Simmer for **10 minutes**.
5. In a bowl, mix flour, baking powder, salt, milk, and melted butter to form a dough.
6. Drop spoonfuls of dough into the pot. Cover and simmer for **15 minutes**, until dumplings are cooked through. Serve hot.

Grilled Teriyaki Pork Chops

Ingredients:

- 4 pork chops
- ½ cup teriyaki sauce
- 2 tbsp soy sauce
- 1 tbsp honey
- 1 tsp garlic powder
- 1 tsp ginger powder
- ½ tsp black pepper
- 1 tbsp olive oil

Instructions:

1. In a bowl, whisk teriyaki sauce, soy sauce, honey, garlic powder, ginger powder, and black pepper.
2. Marinate pork chops for **30 minutes**.
3. Heat a grill to **medium heat**. Brush with olive oil.
4. Grill pork chops for **4-5 minutes per side**, basting with marinade.
5. Let rest for **5 minutes**, then serve with rice or grilled vegetables.

Beef Burrito Bowls

Ingredients:

- 1 lb ground beef
- 1 cup cooked rice
- 1 can (15 oz) black beans, drained and rinsed
- 1 cup corn
- 1 cup cherry tomatoes, chopped
- ½ cup shredded cheddar cheese
- ½ cup sour cream
- ½ cup salsa
- 1 tsp chili powder
- ½ tsp cumin
- ½ tsp salt
- ½ tsp black pepper
- 1 tbsp olive oil

Instructions:

1. Heat olive oil in a pan over **medium heat**. Add ground beef and cook until browned. Drain excess fat.
2. Stir in chili powder, cumin, salt, and black pepper. Cook for **2 more minutes**.
3. In serving bowls, layer rice, beef, black beans, corn, and tomatoes.
4. Top with cheese, sour cream, and salsa. Serve immediately.

Chicken and Broccoli Casserole

Ingredients:

- 2 cups cooked chicken, shredded
- 2 cups broccoli florets, steamed
- 1 can (10.5 oz) cream of chicken soup
- ½ cup sour cream
- 1 cup shredded cheddar cheese
- ½ cup milk
- ½ tsp garlic powder
- ½ tsp onion powder
- ½ cup breadcrumbs
- 2 tbsp butter, melted

Instructions:

1. Preheat oven to **375°F (190°C)**. Grease a baking dish.
2. In a bowl, mix cream of chicken soup, sour cream, milk, garlic powder, and onion powder.
3. Stir in chicken and broccoli. Pour into the baking dish.
4. Top with cheddar cheese. Mix breadcrumbs with melted butter and sprinkle on top.
5. Bake for **20–25 minutes**, until bubbly and golden. Serve warm.

Sweet and Sour Chicken

Ingredients:

- 2 boneless, skinless chicken breasts, cubed
- ½ cup cornstarch
- 2 eggs, beaten
- ½ cup flour
- ½ cup vegetable oil (for frying)
- 1 red bell pepper, chopped
- 1 green bell pepper, chopped
- 1 onion, chopped
- ½ cup pineapple chunks

For the Sauce:

- ½ cup ketchup
- ¼ cup vinegar
- ¼ cup soy sauce
- ⅓ cup brown sugar
- 1 tbsp cornstarch mixed with 2 tbsp water

Instructions:

1. Dredge chicken in cornstarch, dip in eggs, then coat with flour.
2. Heat oil in a pan and fry chicken until golden brown. Drain on paper towels.
3. In a separate pan, sauté peppers, onion, and pineapple for **3 minutes**.
4. In a bowl, whisk ketchup, vinegar, soy sauce, brown sugar, and cornstarch slurry.
5. Pour sauce over vegetables, bring to a boil, then add fried chicken. Toss to coat.
6. Serve hot with rice.

Hawaiian BBQ Chicken

Ingredients:

- 4 boneless, skinless chicken breasts
- ½ cup BBQ sauce
- ¼ cup pineapple juice
- ½ cup pineapple chunks
- 1 tbsp soy sauce
- 1 tsp garlic powder
- ½ tsp black pepper
- 1 tbsp olive oil

Instructions:

1. In a bowl, whisk BBQ sauce, pineapple juice, soy sauce, garlic powder, and black pepper.
2. Marinate chicken for **30 minutes**.
3. Heat oil in a grill pan or outdoor grill over **medium heat**. Grill chicken for **5-6 minutes per side**.
4. During the last 2 minutes, add pineapple chunks to the grill.
5. Serve chicken with grilled pineapple and extra BBQ sauce.

Tuna Casserole

Ingredients:

- 12 oz egg noodles, cooked
- 2 cans (5 oz each) tuna, drained
- 1 can (10.5 oz) cream of mushroom soup
- 1 cup milk
- 1 cup frozen peas
- 1 cup shredded cheddar cheese
- ½ tsp salt
- ½ tsp black pepper
- ½ cup breadcrumbs
- 2 tbsp butter, melted

Instructions:

1. Preheat oven to **375°F (190°C)**.
2. In a large bowl, mix tuna, cream of mushroom soup, milk, peas, cheese, salt, and pepper.
3. Stir in cooked noodles and transfer to a greased baking dish.
4. Mix breadcrumbs with melted butter and sprinkle on top.
5. Bake for **20–25 minutes**, until bubbly and golden.

Spinach and Ricotta Stuffed Shells

Ingredients:

- 12 jumbo pasta shells, cooked
- 1 cup ricotta cheese
- ½ cup mozzarella cheese, shredded
- ¼ cup Parmesan cheese, grated
- 1 cup fresh spinach, chopped
- 1 egg
- 1 tsp garlic powder
- 1½ cups marinara sauce

Instructions:

1. Preheat oven to **375°F (190°C)**.
2. In a bowl, mix ricotta, mozzarella, Parmesan, spinach, egg, and garlic powder.
3. Fill each cooked shell with the mixture and place in a baking dish.
4. Pour marinara sauce over the shells.
5. Cover with foil and bake for **20 minutes**. Remove foil and bake **5 more minutes**.
6. Serve warm with extra Parmesan.

Classic Jambalaya

Ingredients:

- 1 lb andouille sausage, sliced
- 1 lb chicken breast, cubed
- 1 lb shrimp, peeled and deveined
- 1 onion, diced
- 1 bell pepper, diced
- 2 celery stalks, chopped
- 3 cloves garlic, minced
- 1 can (14.5 oz) diced tomatoes
- 3 cups chicken broth
- 1½ cups white rice
- 1 tbsp Cajun seasoning
- ½ tsp thyme
- ½ tsp paprika
- 2 tbsp olive oil
- 2 green onions, chopped

Instructions:

1. Heat olive oil in a large pot over **medium heat**. Cook sausage and chicken until browned. Remove and set aside.
2. In the same pot, sauté onion, bell pepper, celery, and garlic for **5 minutes**.
3. Add diced tomatoes, broth, rice, Cajun seasoning, thyme, and paprika. Bring to a boil.
4. Reduce heat, cover, and simmer for **20 minutes**, stirring occasionally.
5. Stir in shrimp, sausage, and chicken. Cook for **5 more minutes**, until shrimp is pink.
6. Garnish with green onions and serve hot.

Pesto Pasta with Grilled Chicken

Ingredients:

- 2 boneless, skinless chicken breasts
- 2 cups cooked pasta (penne or fettuccine)
- ½ cup basil pesto
- 1 tbsp olive oil
- ¼ cup Parmesan cheese, grated
- ½ cup cherry tomatoes, halved (optional)
- ½ tsp salt
- ½ tsp black pepper

Instructions:

1. Season chicken with salt and pepper.
2. Heat olive oil in a grill pan over **medium heat**. Grill chicken for **5-6 minutes per side**. Slice into strips.
3. Toss cooked pasta with pesto and cherry tomatoes.
4. Top with grilled chicken and Parmesan cheese. Serve warm.

www.ingramcontent.com/pod-product-compliance
Lightning Source LLC
LaVergne TN
LVHW061954070526
838199LV00060B/4113